■SCHOLASTIC

Sight Word Wheels

Reproducible Patterns for Hands-On Wheels That Teach the First 25 Sight Words

by Violet Findley

NEW YORK • TORONTO • LONDON • AUCKLAND • SYDNEY
MEXICO CITY • NEW DELHI • HONG KONG • BUENOS AIRES

Teaching Resources

Written and conceived by Violet Findley
Cover and interior design by Jason Robinson
Interior illustrations by Dana Regan

ISBN-13: 978-0-545-09441-2
ISBN-10: 0-545-09441-0
Copyright © 2008 by Scholastic Inc.
All rights reserved. Published by Scholastic Inc.
Printed in the U.S.A.

2 3 4 5 6 7 8 9 10   40   14 13 12 11 10 09

CONTENTS

Sight Word Wheel Patterns

Introduction

Welcome to Sight Word Wheels! The hands-on wheels in this book will make learning the top 25 sight words easy and fun.

What are sight words? Sight words are little ubiquitous words—*the, of, a, with, you, for*—that appear in print again and again. In fact, research shows that 50 to 75 percent of standard text is comprised of them. Research also shows that these "high-frequency words" seldom adhere to classic spelling patterns, making them very challenging for children to decode. For that reason, most reading specialists advocate rote activities to help young learners commit sight words to memory.

That's where this practical resource comes in! The reproducible wheels on these pages will provide hands-on opportunities for hours of engaging practice—practice that will lead to sight word fluency. And here's more good news: the book is also stocked with entertaining reinforcement activities. We've even included a blank wheel you can customize to explicitly teach whatever sight word—or words—you choose (see page 63).

So what are you waiting for? Put these kid-pleasing learning tools into the hands of your students and watch their reading skills soar!

The 25 wheels in this book teach these essential sight words:

the	in	he	for	we
of	is	she	with	there
and	you	was	at	can
a	that	on	have	an
to	it	are	I	your

Making the Sight Word Wheels

MATERIALS

- paper
- crayons or markers
- scissors
- brass fastener

HOW TO'S

1. Photocopy both parts of the wheel.

2. Color or invite children to color the wheels. (Tip: If you like, paste the pages to oaktag and/or laminate them for added durability.)

3. Cut out both wheels. Cut out the windows along the dashed lines.

4. Place the window wheel on top of the picture wheel. Align the dots in the center as shown.

5. Push a brass fastener through the dots and open to secure. Now you're ready to turn to learn!

6. For extra practice, invite students to write the sight words they are learning on the sight word stationery (see page 10.)

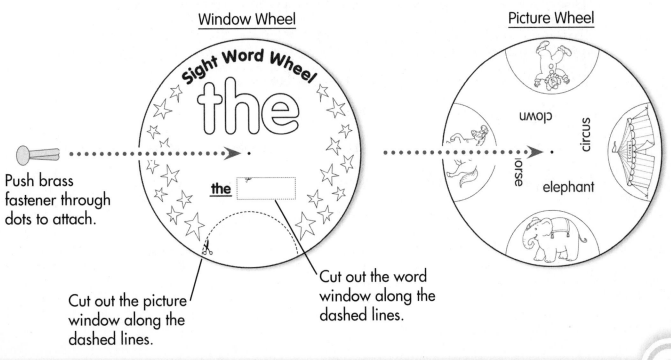

Window Wheel

Sight Word Wheel

the

the

Picture Wheel

clown

circus

horse

elephant

Push brass fastener through dots to attach.

Cut out the picture window along the dashed lines.

Cut out the word window along the dashed lines.

Sight Word Games and Activities

Use these easy ideas to give children hands-on experiences with the sight words they are learning.

Transition Time Sight Words

You can squeeze in sight word practice at any time of day with these quick ideas.

Lining Up: Write sight words on index cards, creating two matching sets. Tape one set of cards to the floor in a row where children usually line up. Place the other set in a box. Each time children need to line up, have them choose a card from the box. Then challenge children to line up by standing on the spot with the matching word. Alternatively, you can give each child a word card and challenge children to line up by putting themselves in alphabetical order.

Find a Partner: Write pairs of matching sight words on index cards and place the cards in a bag or box. When children need to find partners for an activity, have each child pick a card. Children who picked the same card can find each other and work together.

Snack Time: Create sight word place mats by writing target words on sheets of construction paper and laminating them or covering them with clear contact paper. Write matching words on index cards. Before snack time, place the mats on the table and give each child a random word card. Invite children to find their place at the table by finding the matching word on a place mat.

Cleaning Up: When it's time to clean up, call out sight words one at a time. Have children spell out the word, count the number of letters, and then put away the same number of items.

Time to Go: When it's time to pack up, avoid the cubby crush by giving each child an index card with a sight word. Invite small groups to go to their cubbies by calling out different categories, for instance: everyone whose word contains the letter *p*; everyone who has a five-letter word; everyone whose word begins with a *t*; and so on.

Touchy-Feely Spelling

Tactile learners will benefit from sensory writing experiences. You can squirt shaving cream on a cookie sheet and have children write sight words in the cream using a finger. If they make a mistake, they can "erase" by smoothing the cream over with their palm. You can also fill a plastic tub with damp sand and have children spell words using a dowel. As a third option, fill a zip-close sandwich bag halfway with tinted hair gel. Write sight words on large index cards and have children place the gel bag on top of a card. Children can use their finger to trace the letters in the gel.

Sight Word Scavenger Hunt

Give each child a list of target words, a stack of old magazines, a sheet of construction paper, scissors, and glue. Then have children hunt through the magazines for the words on their list. Each time they find a word, they can cut it out and glue it on the paper. When finished, children will have a sight word collage, most likely filled with lots of different fonts and colors.

Silly Sentence of the Day

Write target sight words on small slips of paper and place them in a bag. Each day, have a different volunteer choose three to five words from the bag (depending on children's skill level). Then have the whole class work together to write a silly sentence containing all the words. For instance, if a child draws the words *want, jump,* and *funny,* the sentence might be: *We want to jump like funny frogs.* Write the sentence on a sheet of chart paper, using a different color marker for the target words. You can add a new sentence to your chart each day.

Hop 'n' Type

This activity is fun for all children, and especially good for kinesthetic learners. On an old bed sheet or shower curtain liner, use a permanent marker to write letters in squares to make a giant QWERTY computer keyboard. (You can include only the letter keys, leaving out the numerals and punctuation marks.) Use masking tape to attach the keyboard securely to the floor. Then let children take off their shoes and have them line up behind the keyboard. As each child steps up to the keyboard, call out a random sight word and have the child hop on the appropriate "keys" to spell out the word! Continue until each child has had a turn.

Sight Word Scramble

Use alphabet letter cards to play this fun game. Choose a "secret" sight word and gather the appropriate letters to spell the word. Then call a number of children up to the front (the same number of children as letters in the word). Huddle up with children and whisper the secret word, giving each child a letter card. Then have children stand in a row facing the group, and hold their letter cards in front of them in mixed-up order. Children in the audience then take turns asking one child at a time to move to a different spot; for instance: *Keisha, go stand between Andres and Jake.* Then the next child gets to move a letter. Children can move only one letter on their turn. Have children continue to rearrange the letter holders until they're standing in the correct order. Once the word is unscrambled, choose a new sight word and a new team of letter holders.

Sight Word Tic Tac Toe

Draw a tic tac toe grid on the board and divide the class into two teams, X's and O's. Fill each space in the grid with a sight word. The game is played just like regular tic tac toe, with members of each team choosing a space to cover. In order to mark the space with an X or an O, the team member must read the word in that space correctly. The team that gets three X's or O's in a row wins the game.

Shake-a-Word

To prepare this game, get a clean, empty egg carton and small self-stick labels. Write sight words on 12 labels and stick one in each cup of the carton. Then place a number cube inside the carton. In groups of two to four, have children play the game as follows. The first player closes the carton and shakes it. He or she then opens up the carton and notes what number is facing up on the cube. The child then removes the cube and reads the sight word that's printed in the cup in which the cube landed. If the child reads the word correctly, he or she earns the number of points shown on the cube. Then it is the next player's turn. Children can play for a set number of rounds or as time permits.

Sight Word Baseball

Gather in an open area and create four "bases" by placing beanbags or books on the floor to make a mini–baseball diamond. Write on index cards any sight words you'd like to reinforce and divide the class into two teams. You can play the game similarly to regular baseball. Have one team go up to "bat" by lining up behind home plate. "Pitch" a word to the first player by holding up an index card. If the player gets a "hit" by reading the word correctly, he or she moves to first base and it is the next hitter's turn. For each word a hitter reads correctly, each child on the diamond moves forward one base. When a child gets to home base, a point is earned for that team. Each time a child misses a word, the team gets an "out." Three outs, and it's the next team's turn! You can continue to play the game for a set number of "innings."

Sentence-Builder Hangman

This version of "hangman" reinforces both spelling and how words are used in context. Choose a "mystery" sight word and build a sentence around it, writing blanks for the letters of the target word. For instance, for the word *around*, you might write "The dog chased the cat __ __ __ __ __ __ the yard." Just like regular hangman, children guess one letter at a time. If the letter appears in the word, write it in the appropriate space. If not, add one body part to the "hangman." Children try to solve the word before the hangman's body is complete!

Sight Word Blotto

This game adds an element of chance, so even a beginning reader can get the most points. In advance, write sight words you'd like to reinforce on index cards. For about every ten cards, create a "Blotto" card by writing "Blotto!" in big red letters. Set an amount of time to play (about 10 to 15 minutes). Then place all the cards in a bag or box and have children take turns coming up to pick a card. If the child can read the word, he or she keeps the card. If not, it goes back in the box. Children will begin to accumulate cards, but any child who draws a Blotto card must place all of his or her cards back in the box and start from scratch! When time is up, children can count their cards to see who has the most.

Sight Word Bingo

Write 20 to 25 sight words on the board, and write the same words on separate index cards. Then give each child a bingo grid with 16 squares. To create their game boards, children can choose any 16 words from the board and write one in each square. Give children counters or dried beans to use as markers. To play, place the index cards in a paper bag and pull out one at a time at random. If children have the word on their board, they can cover it with a marker. The first child to get four in a row (vertically, horizontally, or diagonally) calls out "Bingo!" Then have children clear their boards and play another round.

Go Fish

Create a deck of cards by writing 26 sight words on separate index cards. Write each word twice on each card, and cut the cards in half to make a deck of 52 cards. Children can play the game in groups of three to six. Each player gets five cards, and the remaining cards are placed facedown in the middle. The first player chooses a word from his or her hand and asks another player for the matching word card. If the player has the card, he or she hands it over. If not, that player says, "Go fish," and the first player picks the top card from the middle deck. If the drawn card makes a pair, the player places the pair on the table. If not, the player keeps the card and it is the next player's turn. Play continues until one player runs out of cards or the middle deck is used up.

Sight Word Wheels

Sight Word Wheel

the

<u>the</u>

Assembled Wheel

Sight Word Wheel

the

<u>the</u> elephant

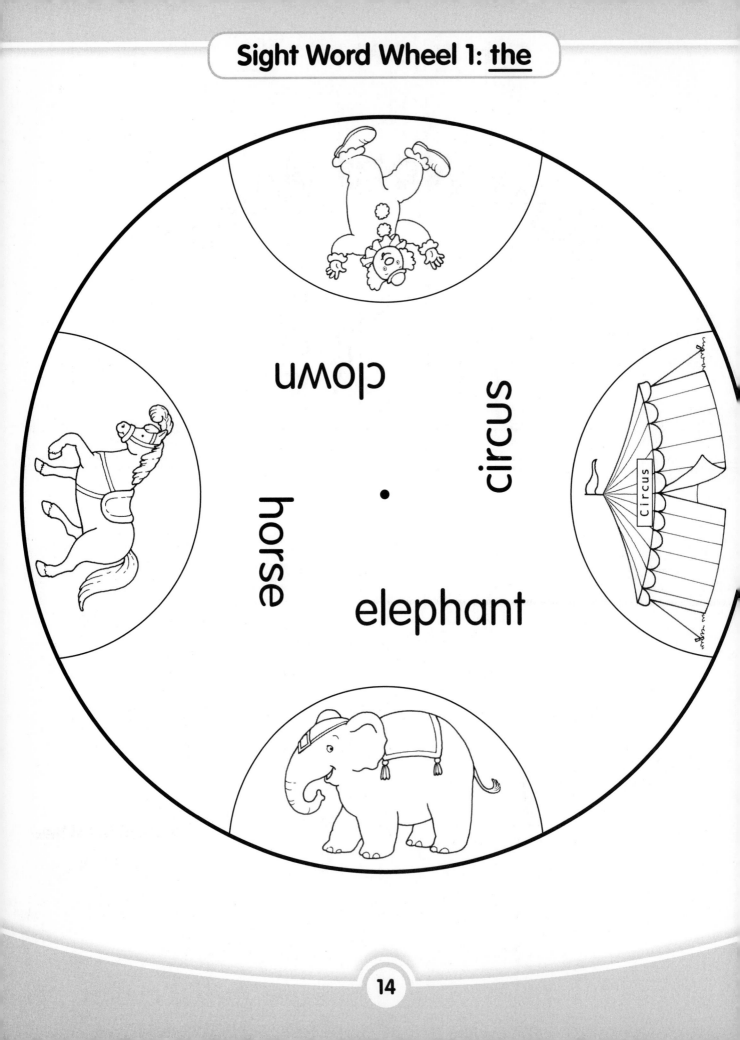

clown

circus

horse

elephant

Sight Word Wheel

of

made **of**

Assembled Wheel

clay

paper

blocks

buttons

Sight Word Wheel

and

dog **<u>and</u>**

Assembled Wheel

Sight Word Wheel

and

dog **and** bone

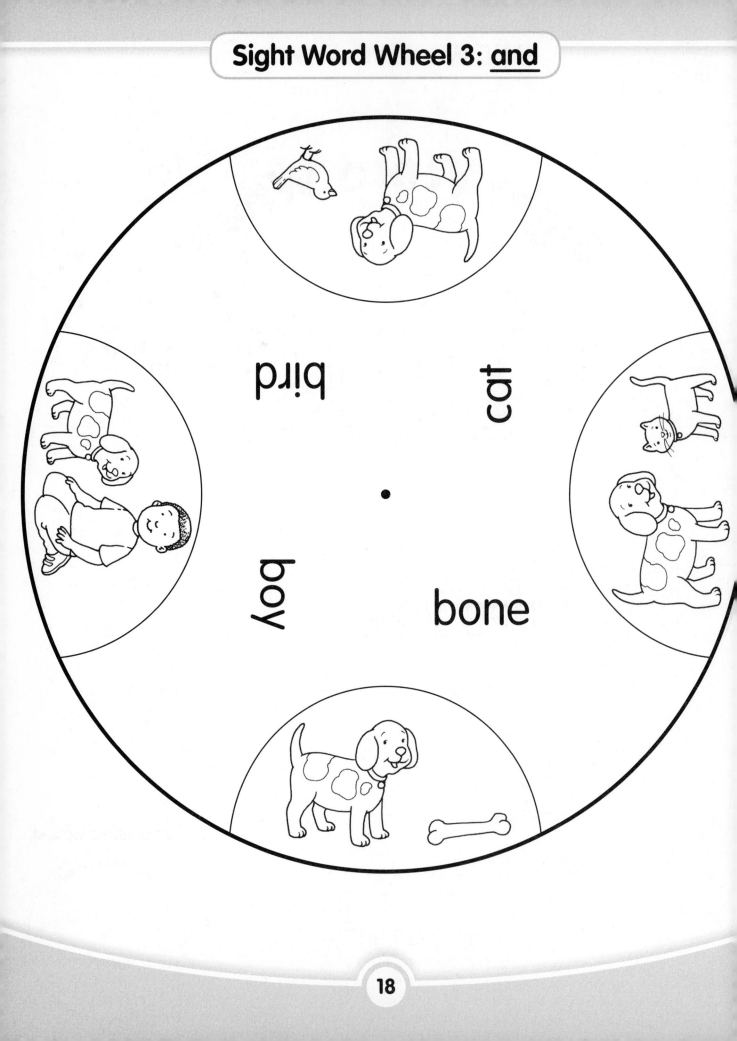

bird

cat

boy

bone

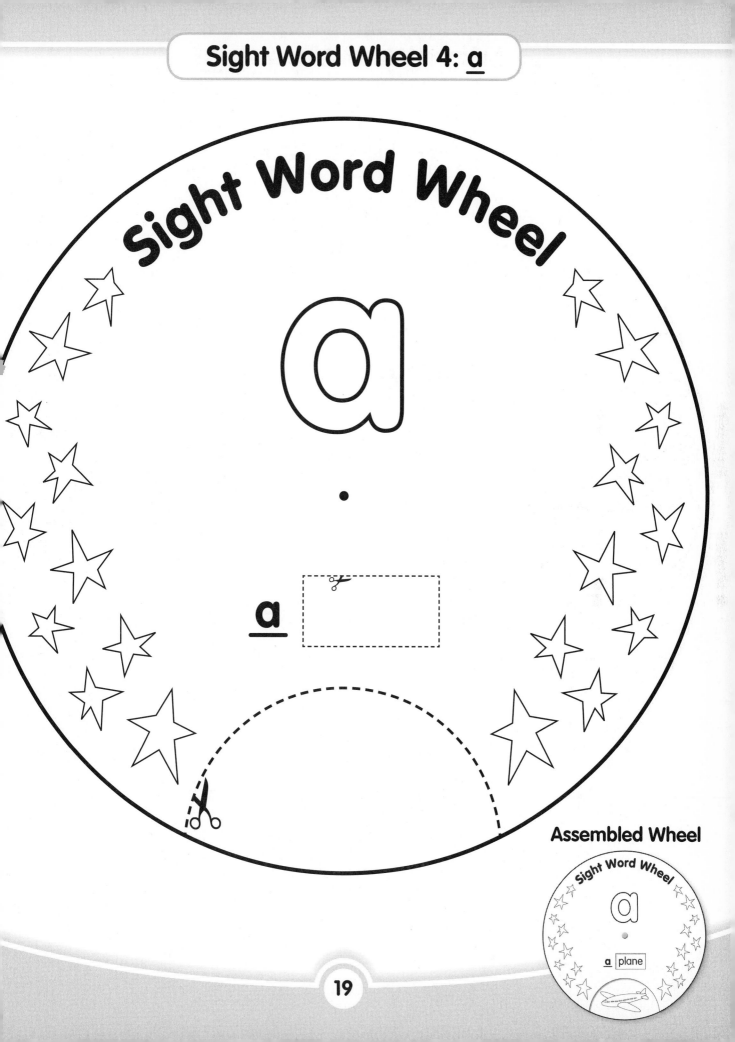

Sight Word Wheel

a

<u>a</u>

Assembled Wheel

Sight Word Wheel

a

<u>a</u> plane

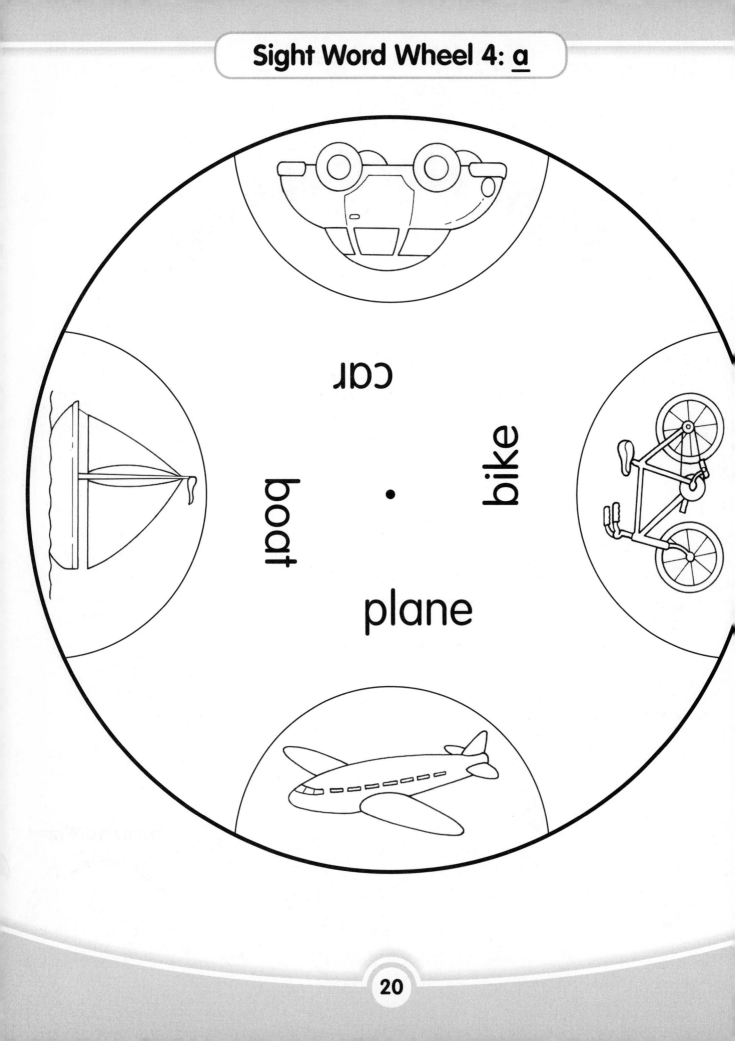

car

boat

bike

plane

Sight Word Wheel

to

<u>to</u> the

Assembled Wheel

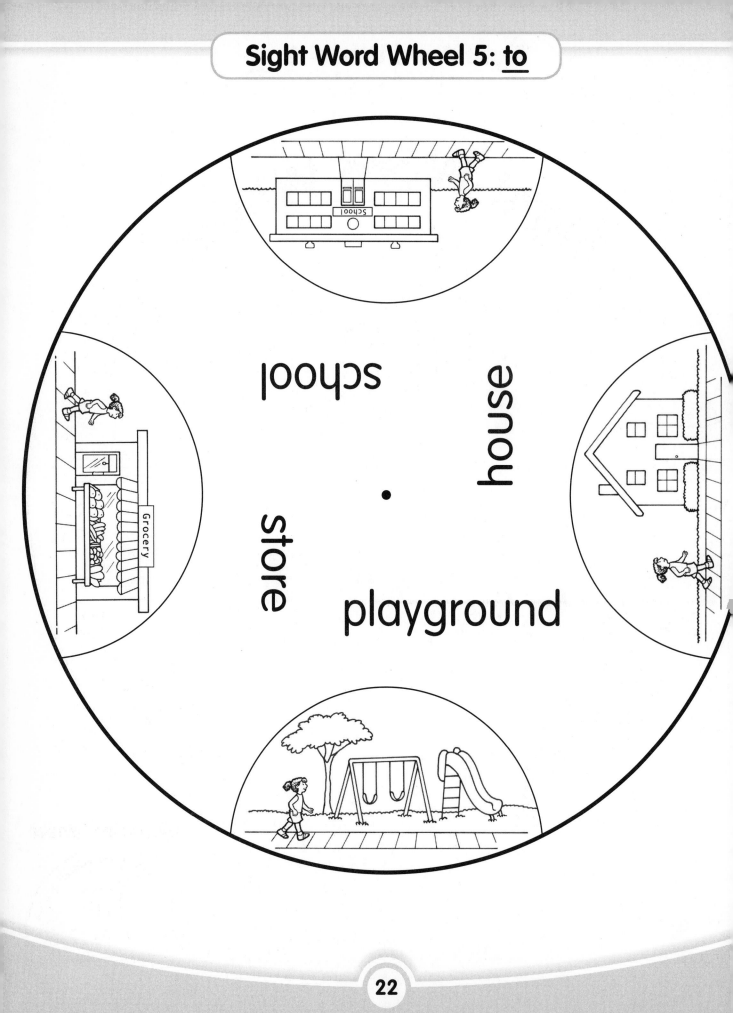

Sight Word Wheel

in

pig **<u>in</u>** a [ ]

Assembled Wheel

Sight Word Wheel

in

pig **in** a [hat]

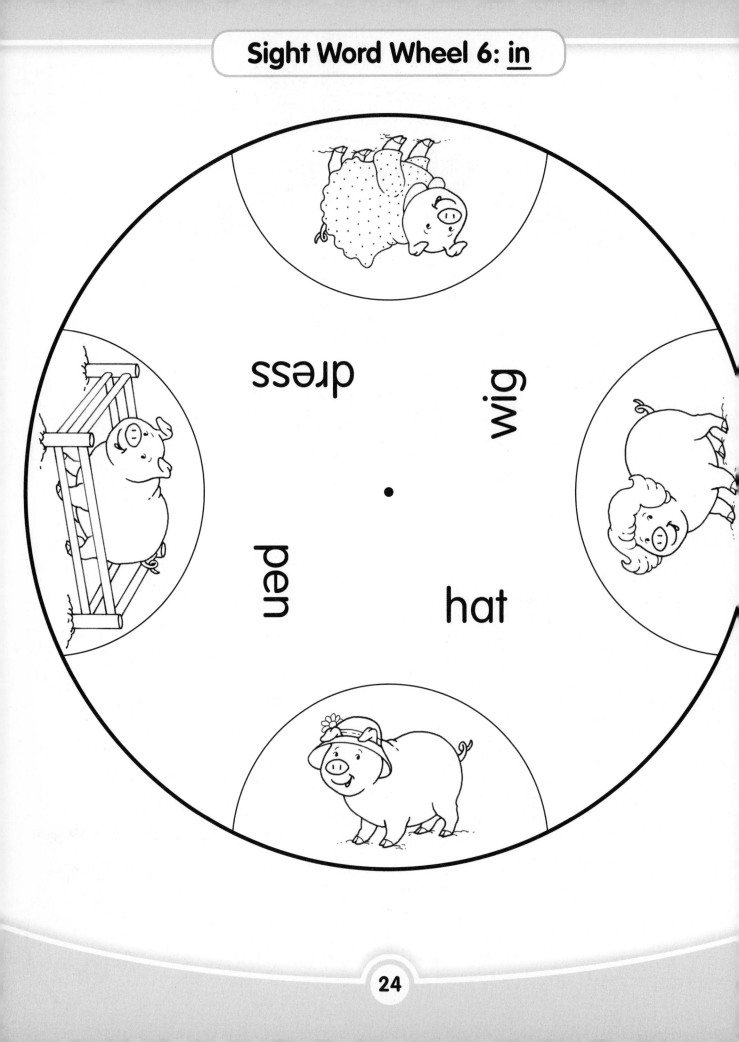

dress

wig

pen

hat

Sight Word Wheel

is

There **is**

Assembled Wheel

Sight Word Wheel

is

There **is** salad.

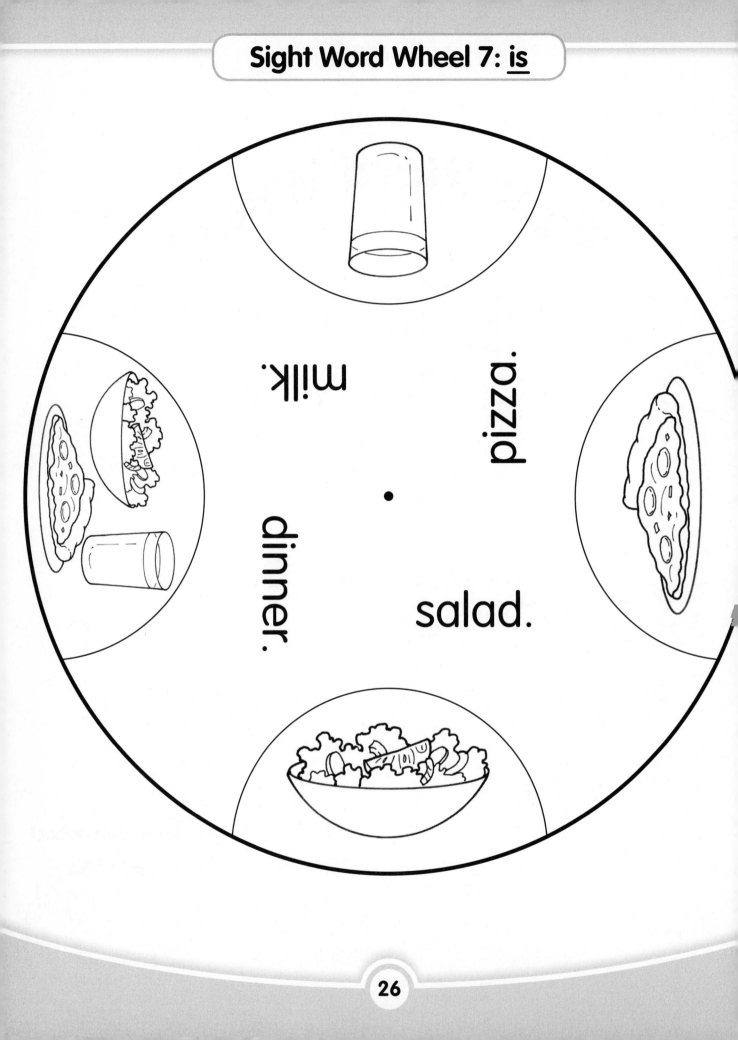

milk.

pizza.

dinner.

salad.

Sight Word Wheel

YOU

Are **you**

Assembled Wheel

Sight Word Wheel 8: <u>you</u>

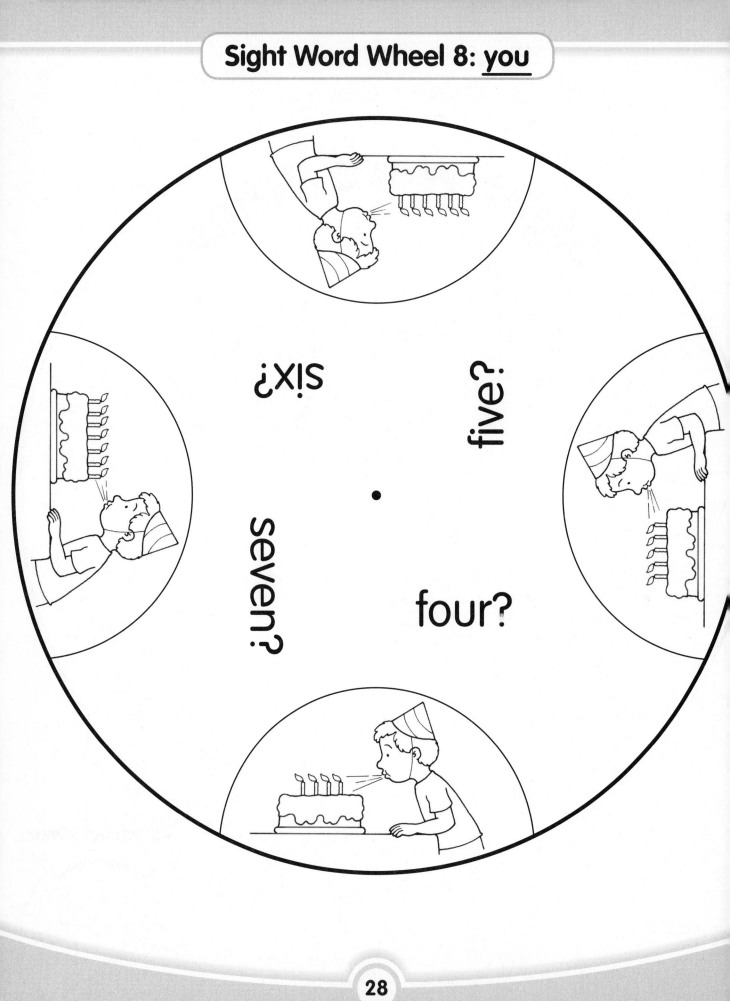

six?

five?

seven?

four?

Sight Word Wheel

that

<u>that</u>

Assembled Wheel

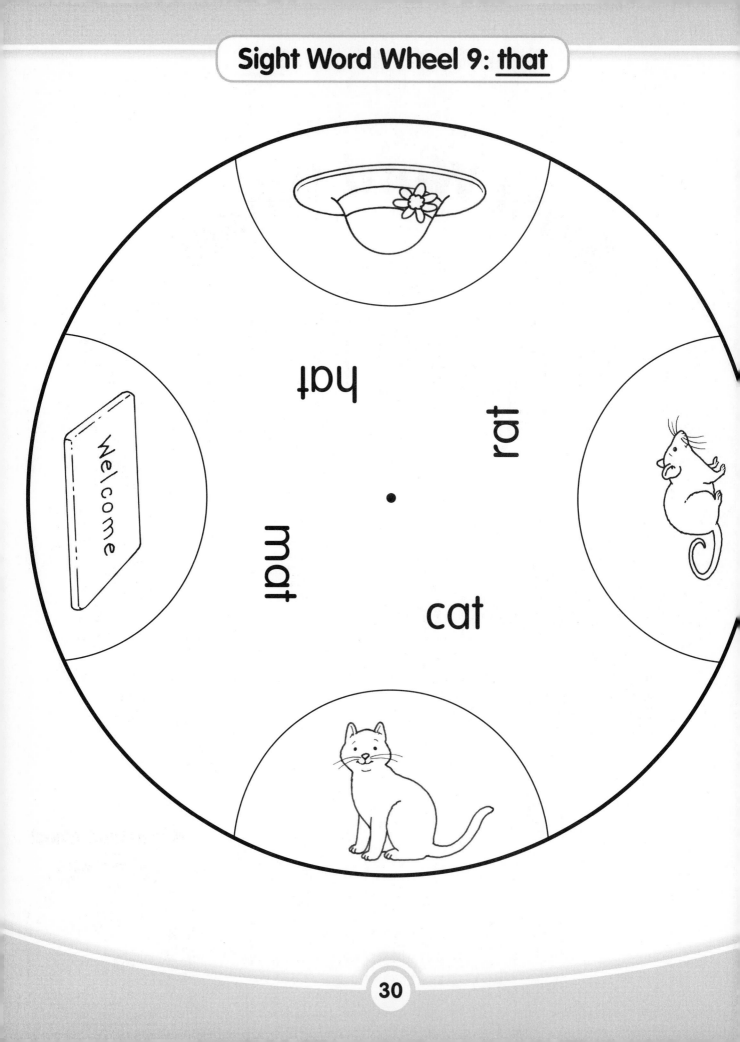

Sight Word Wheel

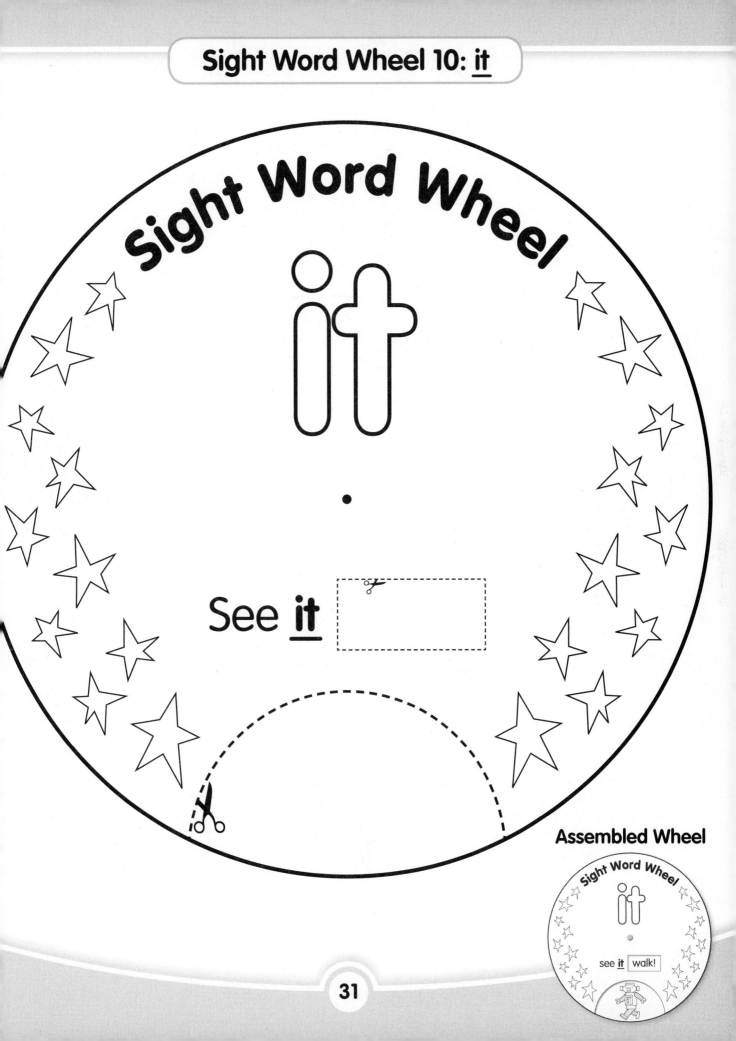

See <u>it</u>

Assembled Wheel

Sight Word Wheel

see <u>it</u> walk!

jump!

talk!

sleep!

walk!

Sight Word Wheel

he

Is <u>he</u>

Assembled Wheel

Sight Word Wheel

he

Is <u>he</u> | hot?

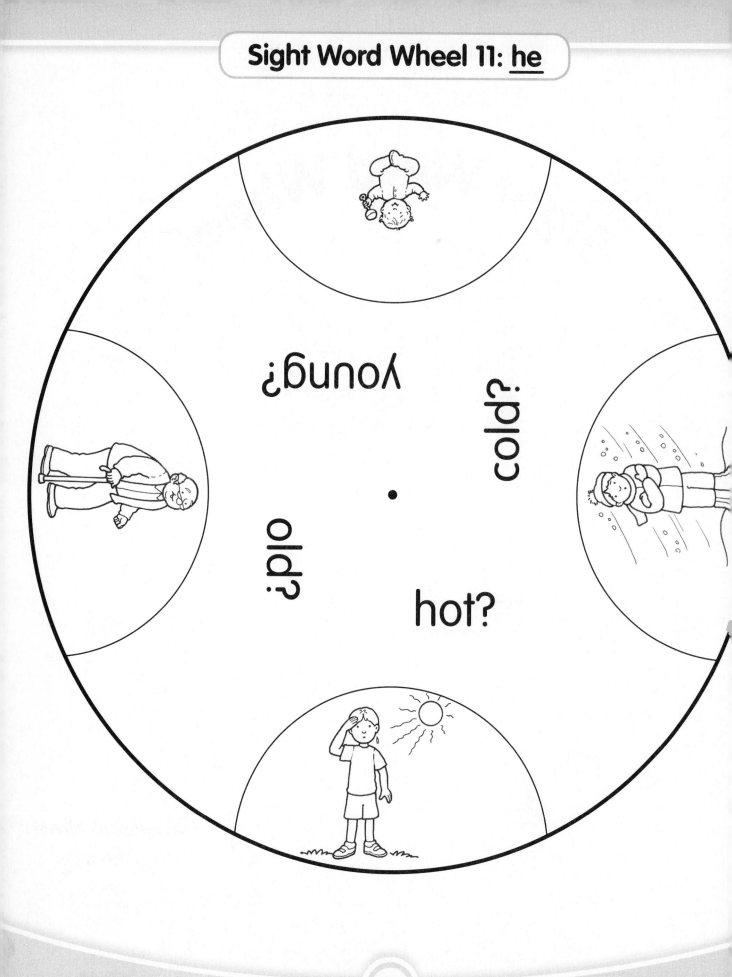

young?

cold?

old?

hot?

Sight Word Wheel

she

Is <u>she</u>

Assembled Wheel

Sight Word Wheel

she

Is <u>she</u> happy?

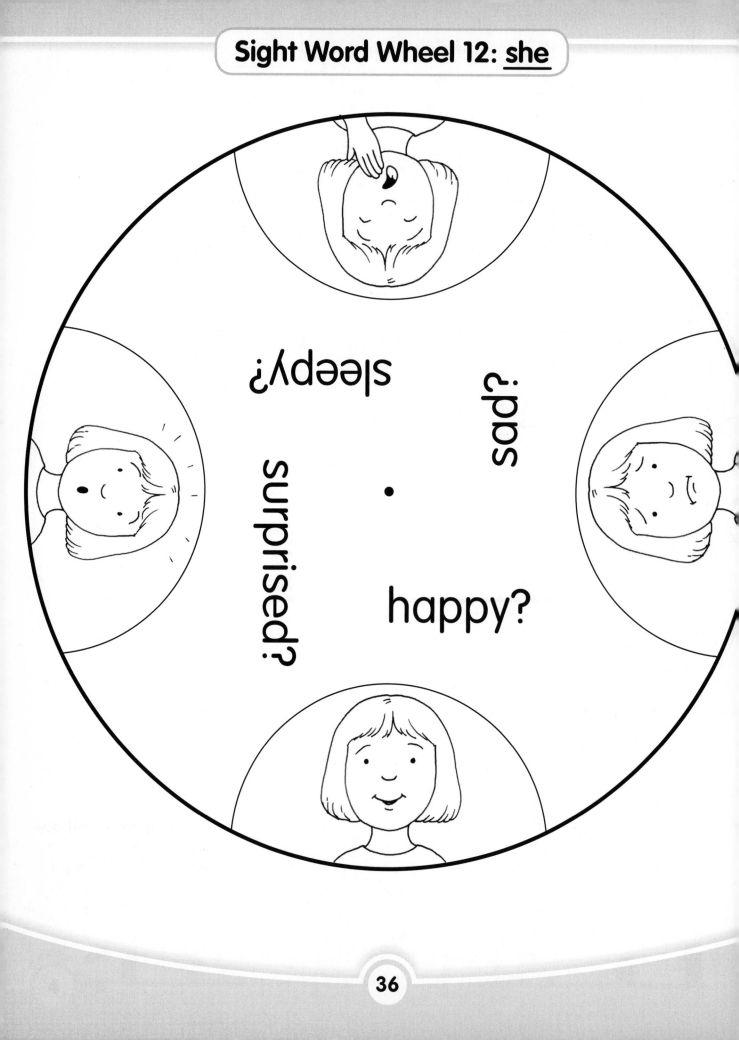

sleepy?

sad?

surprised?

happy?

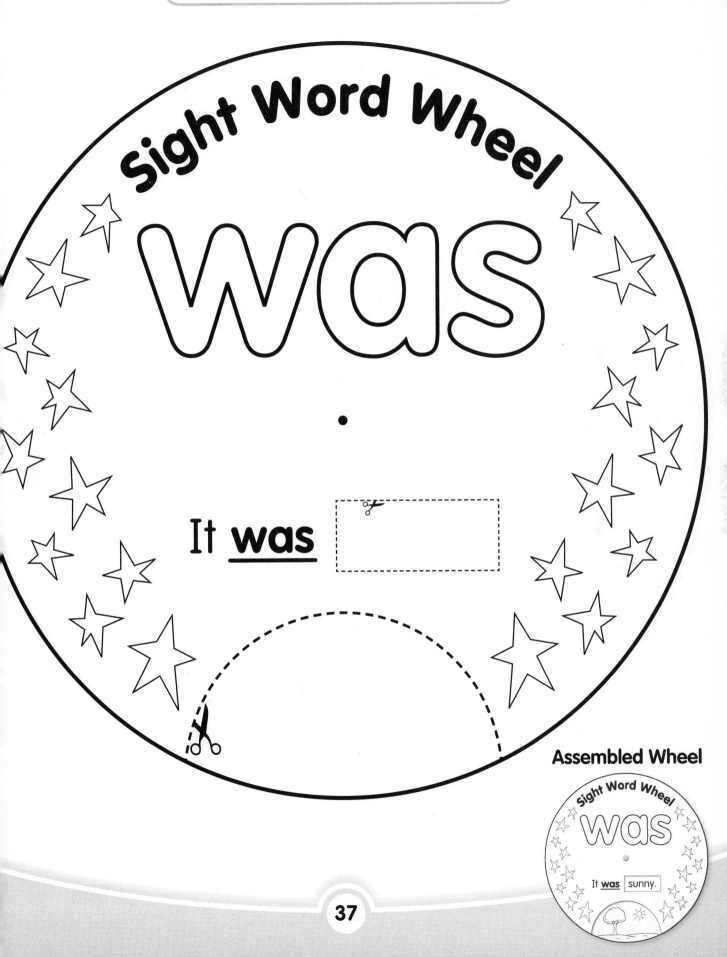

Sight Word Wheel

was

It <u>**was**</u>

Assembled Wheel

rainy.

cloudy.

snowy.

sunny.

Sight Word Wheel

on

hat **<u>on</u>** a

Assembled Wheel

Sight Word Wheel

on

hat <u>on</u> a cat

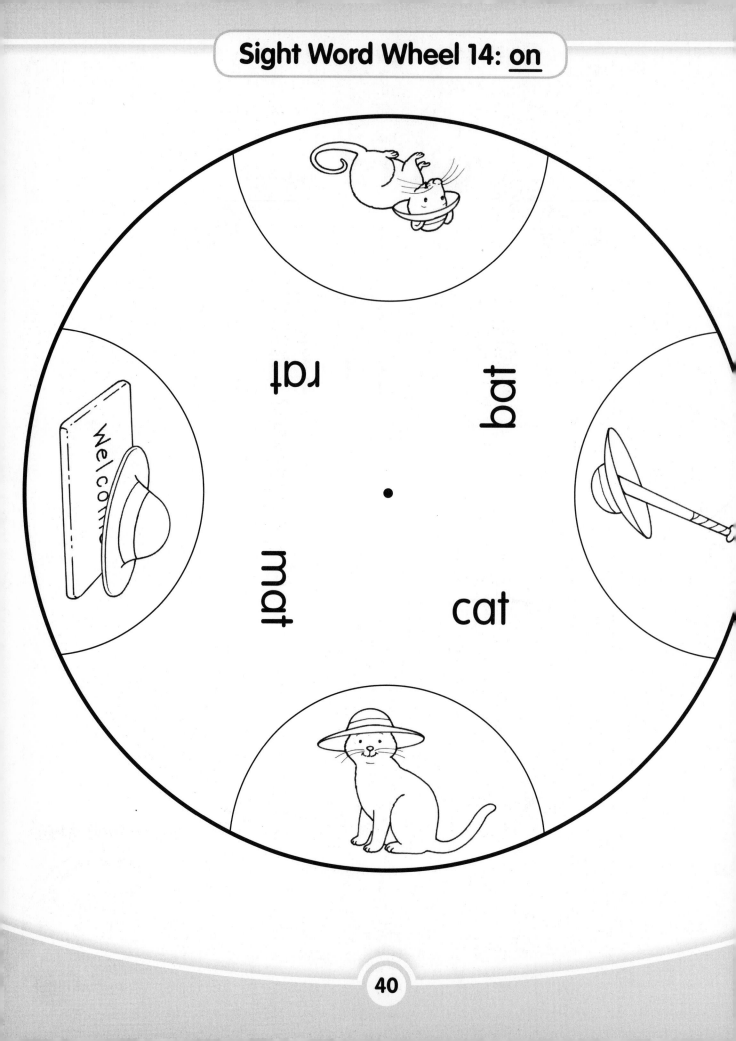

Sight Word Wheel

are

Here **<u>are</u>**

Assembled Wheel

Sight Word Wheel

are

They **are** circles.

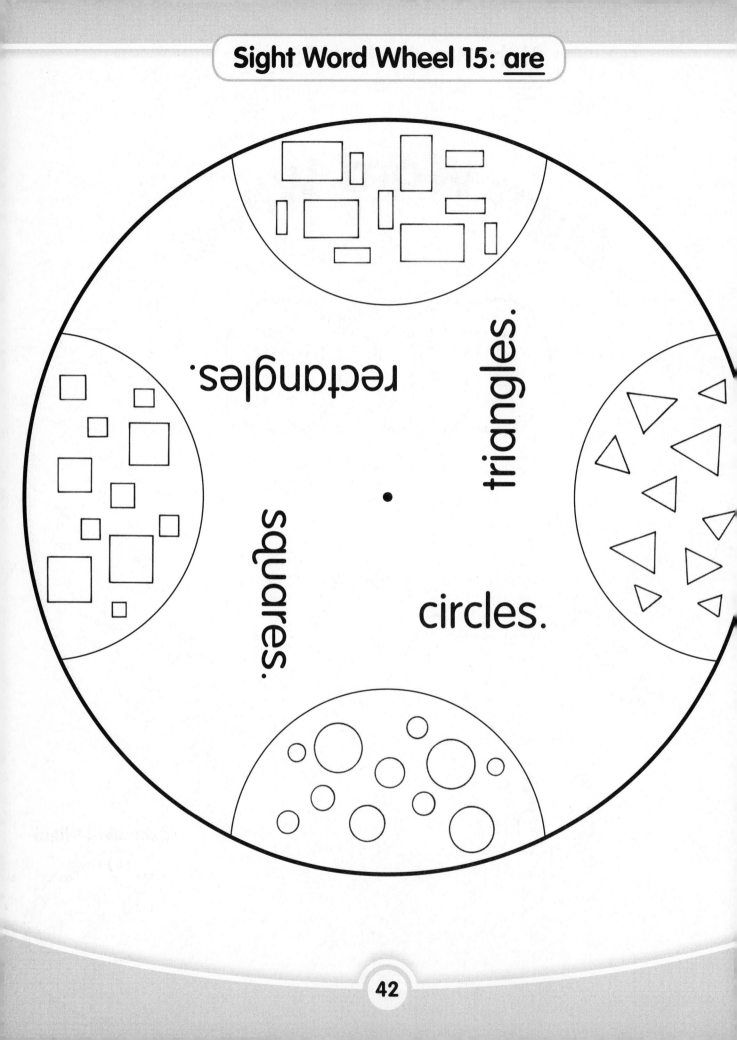

rectangles.

triangles.

squares.

circles.

Sight Word Wheel

for

for a

Assembled Wheel

Sight Word Wheel

for

for a | dog

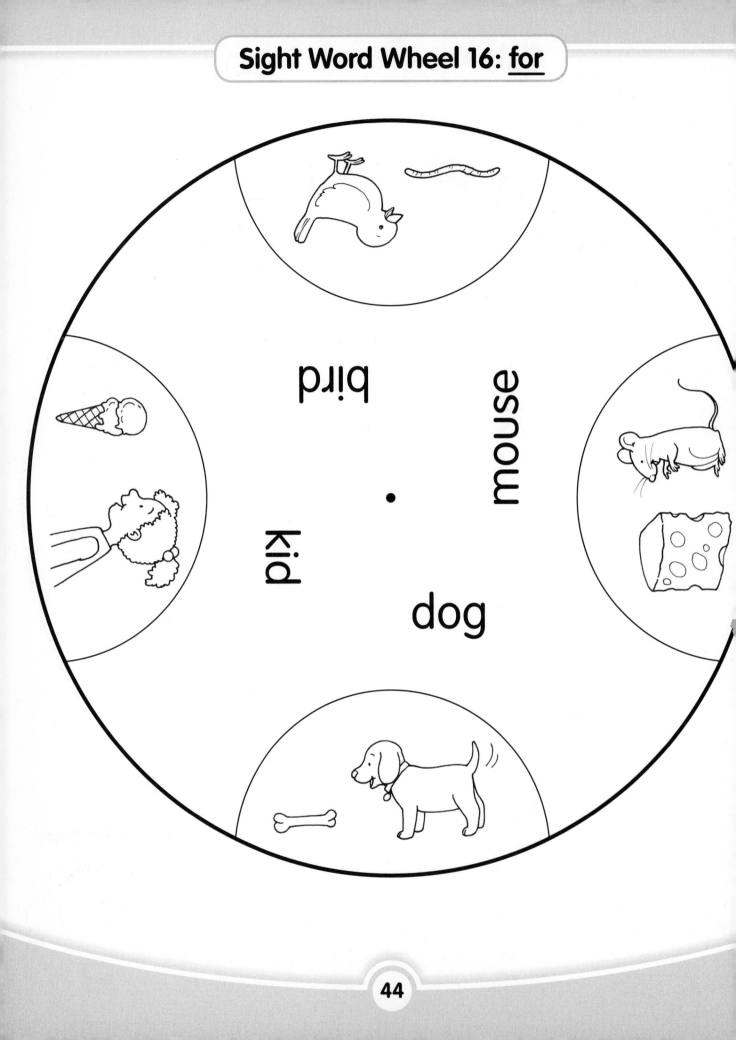

bird

mouse

kid

dog

Sight Word Wheel

with

ham __with__

Assembled Wheel

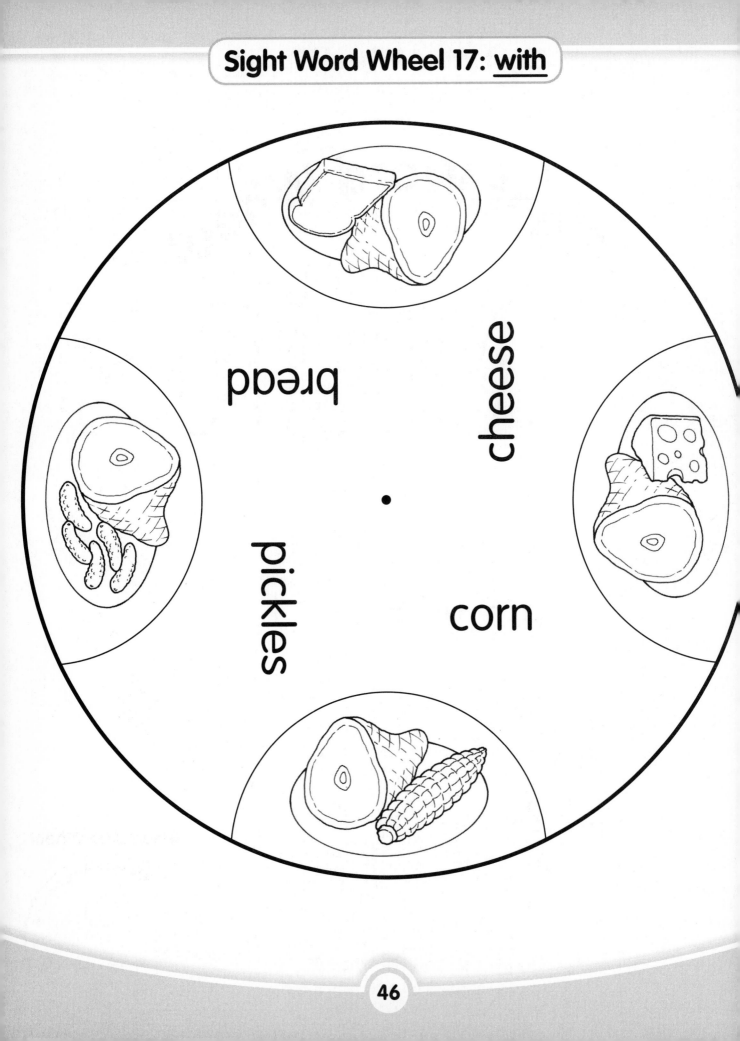

bread

cheese

pickles

corn

Sight Word Wheel

at

<u>at</u> the [✂]

Sight Word Wheel

at

<u>at</u> the | store

Assembled Wheel

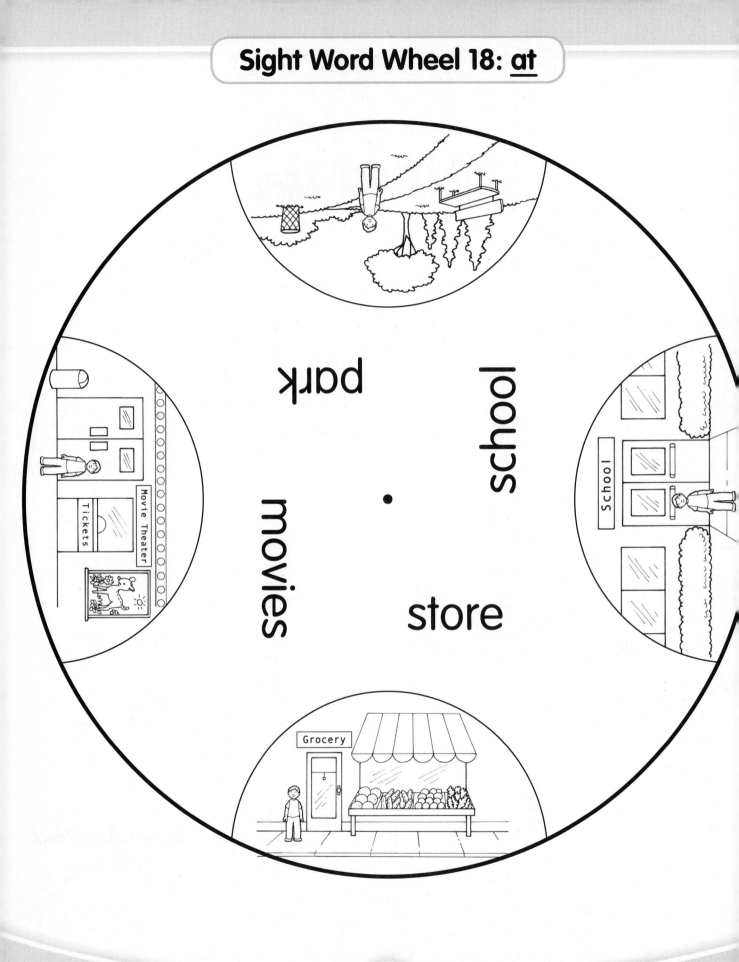

park

school

movies

store

Sight Word Wheel

have

I **have** a [ ]

Assembled Wheel

Sight Word Wheel

have

I **have** a cow.

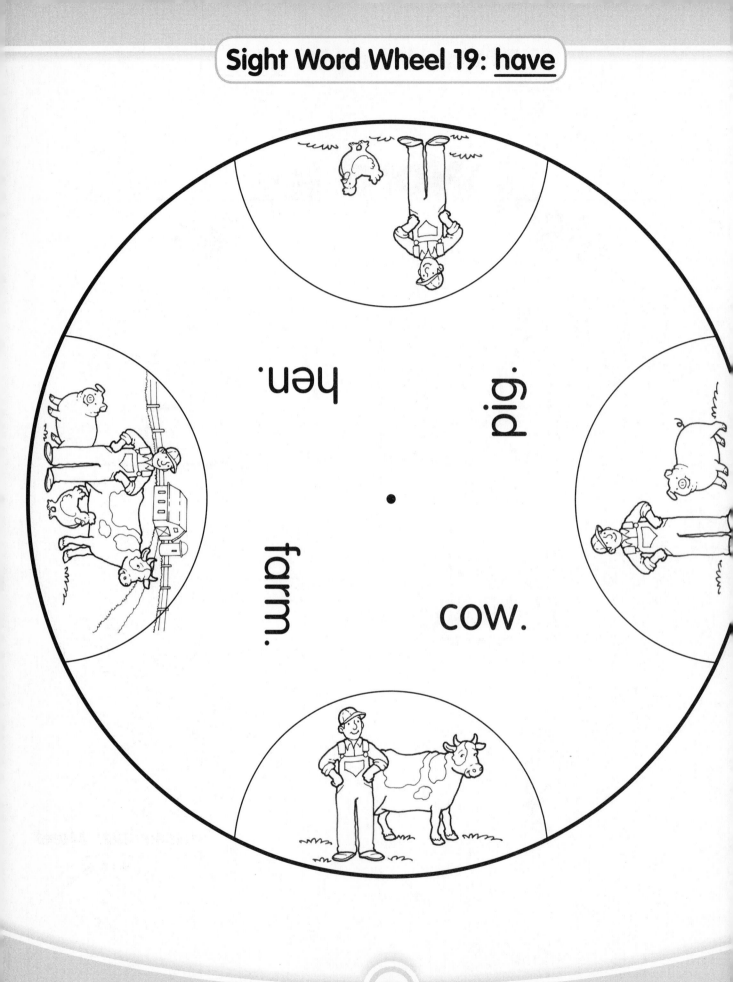

pig.

hen.

cow.

farm.

Sight Word Wheel

I

<u>I</u> love

Assembled Wheel

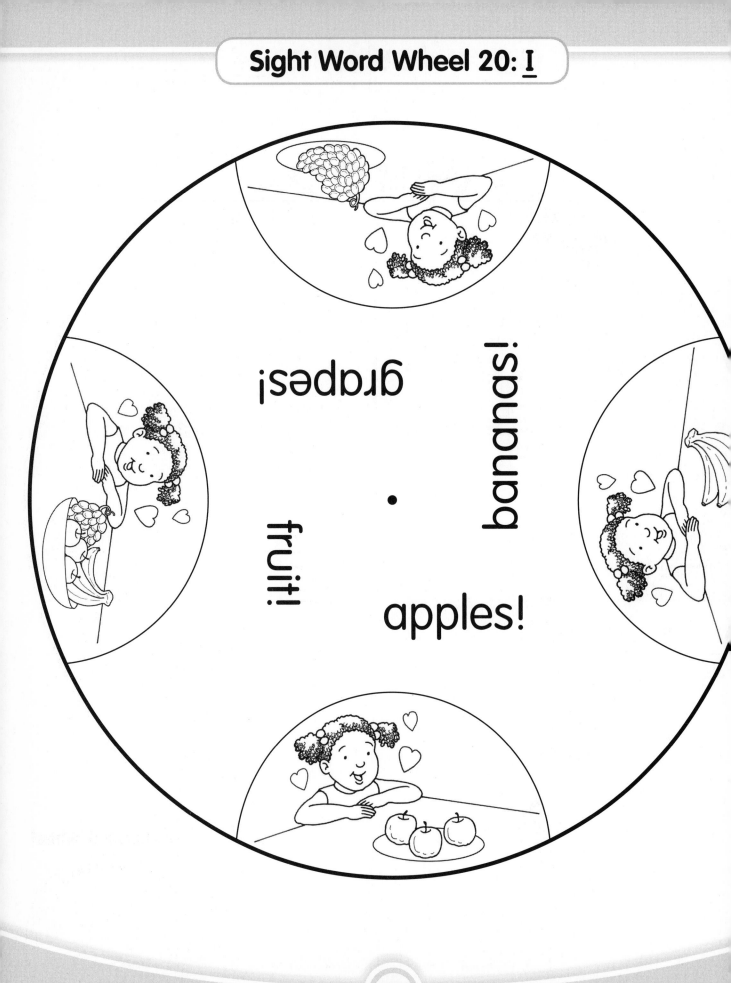

grapes!

bananas!

fruit!

apples!

Sight Word Wheel

we

Today <u>we</u> ✂

Assembled Wheel

Sight Word Wheel

we

Today <u>we</u> read.

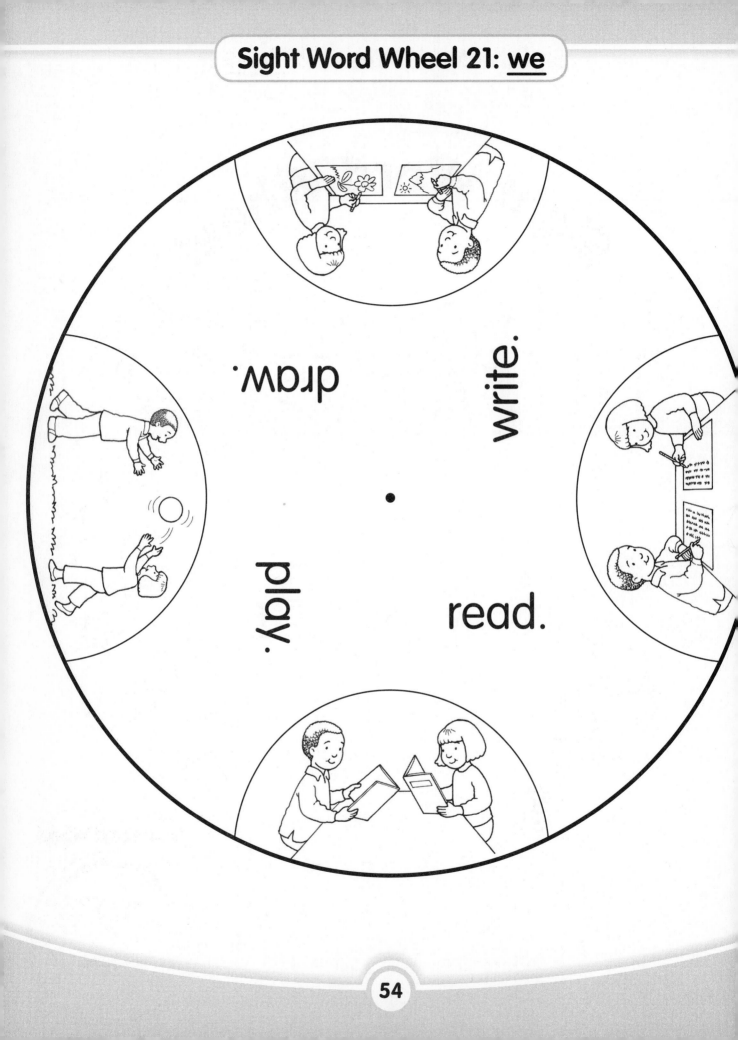

draw.

write.

play.

read.

Sight Word Wheel

there

is **<u>there</u>**.

Assembled Wheel

Sight Word Wheel

there

Red is **there**.

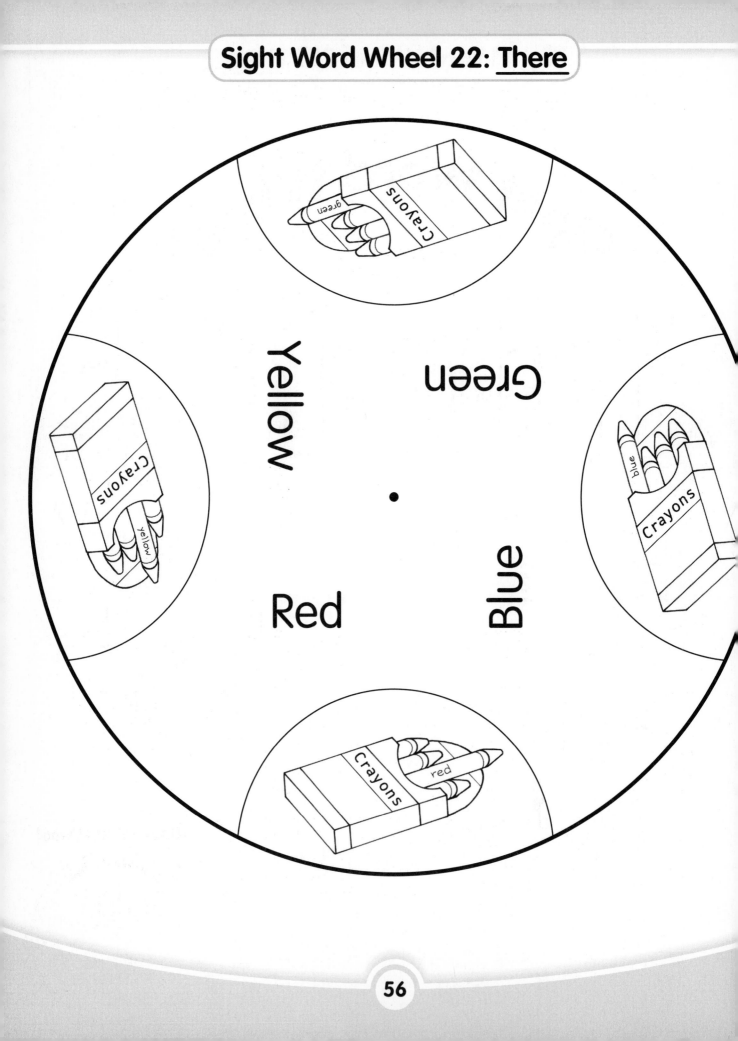

Sight Word Wheel

can

I __can__

Assembled Wheel

throw!

jump!

catch!

run!

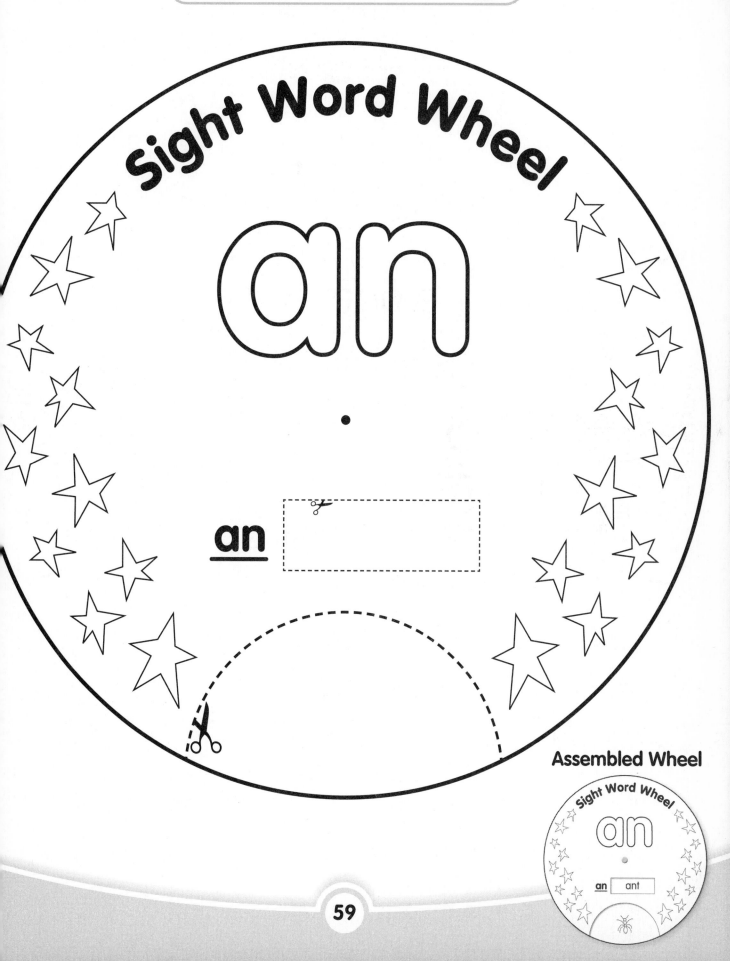

Sight Word Wheel

an

<u>an</u>

Assembled Wheel

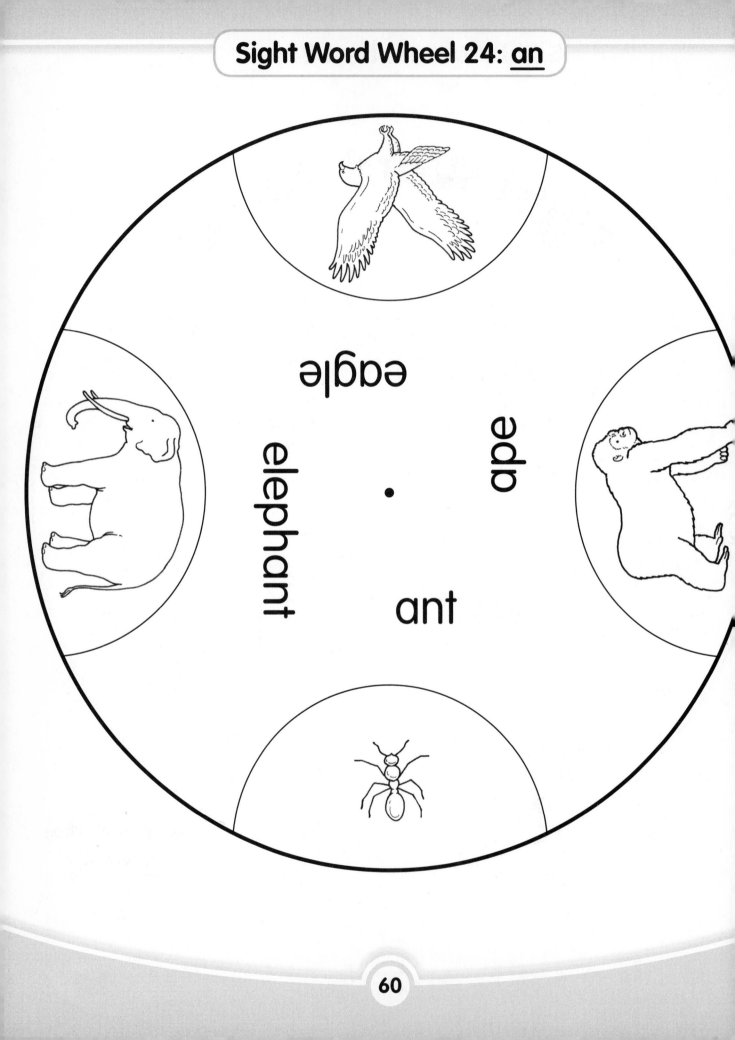

eagle

ape

elephant

ant

Sight Word Wheel

your

your <u>your</u>

Assembled Wheel

Sight Word Wheel

your

your | toys

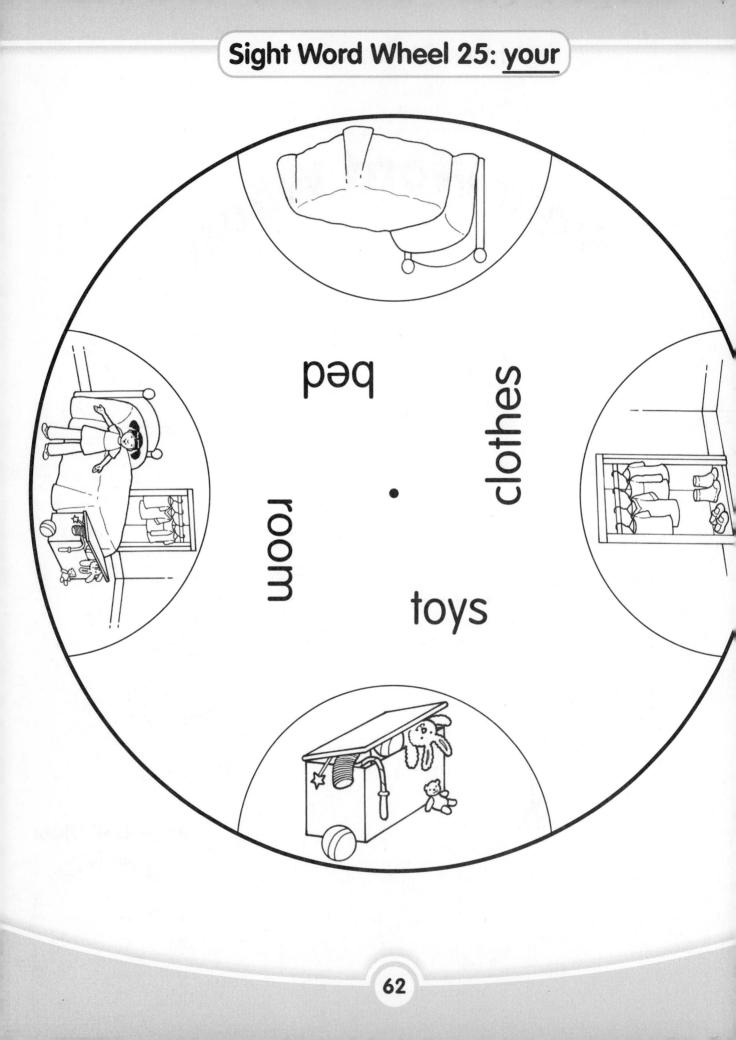

Sight Word Wheel

Assembled Wheel

Sight Word Wheel: <u>blank</u>

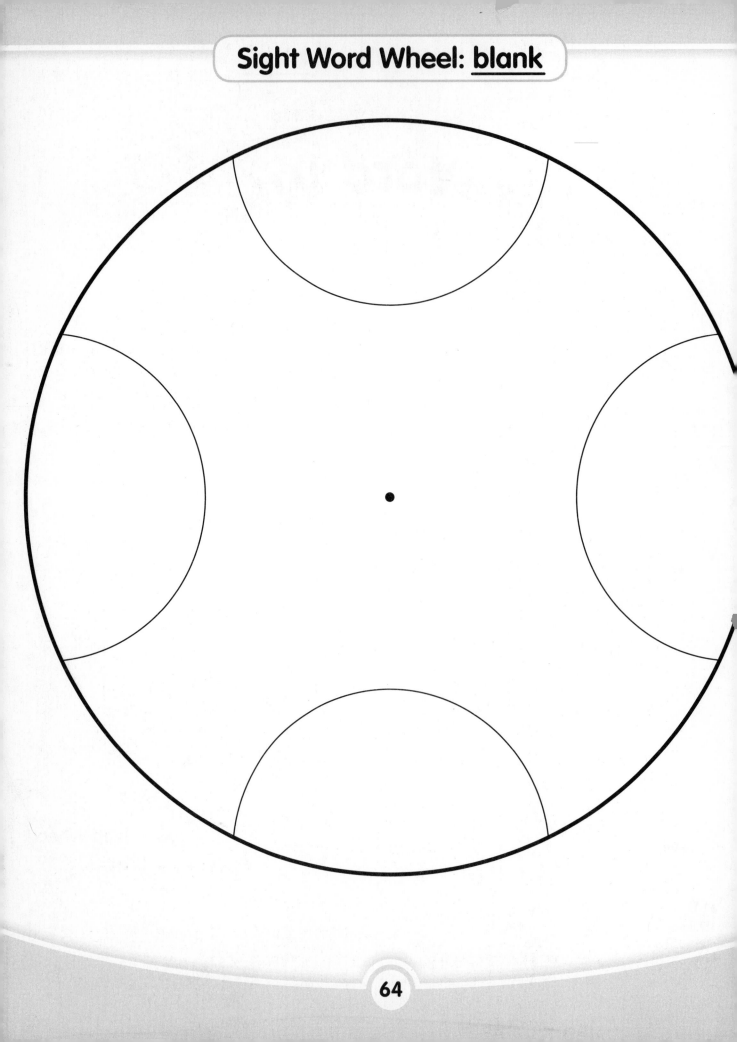